Good2go
NOTARY PUBLIC
RECORD BOOK 2

——— Published by ———
Good2go Publishing
P.O. Box 758, Laveen AZ 85339
www.good2gopublishing.com
Made in the USA

I0057996

THIS IS A RECORD OF NOTARIAL ACTS FORM

_____

Date

to

_____

Date

Property of:

NOTARY PUBLIC

NOTARY PUBLIC COMMISSION INFORMATION

Name: _____   _____
         Printed Official Signature   Signed Official Signature

Address: _____

Telephone Bus: _____

Home: _____

City, State, Zip: _____

Notary Public Commission Expires: _____

Commission Number: _____   Bond Number: _____

Notary Public Commission Expires: _____

Commission Number: _____   Bond Number: _____

Notary Public Commission Expires: _____

Commission Number: _____   Bond Number: _____

Name: of My Bonding Company: _____

Address: _____

Telephone: _____

City, State, Zip: _____

Page 1	DATE NOTARIZED	TYPE OF NOTARIZATION	DATE OF DOCUMENT	TYPE OF DOCUMENT	SIGNATURE OF INDIVIDUAL	
					PRINTED	SIGNATURE
1						
2						
3						
4						
5						
6						
7						
8						
9						
10						
11						
12						
13						
14						
15						
16						
17						
18						
19						
20						

NOTARY PUBLIC COMMISSION INFORMATION

Most states require that each notary public keep a bound record book in which they record the important information pertaining notarial acts they perform. The following basic information is required; however, laws may very in different states. Each notary public should be informed of information required by their own state.

- Date of the acknowledgment/notarization.
- Type of acknowledgment/notarization.
- Date of document.
- Type of document.
- Name/signature of individual.
- Residence of individual.
- Detailed identification of individual.
- Name and residence of witnesses.
- Identification of witnesses.
- Any other pertinent information regarding the document, or individuals signing the document.
- Fee charged for notary public service (should not exceed those fee permitted by your state law.

Special Note

California's Lost Angeles Country, requires signers of deeds affecting real property is the country to leave a right thumb print in a Notary's Journal.

ADDRESS OF INDIVIDUAL	DETAILED IDENTIFICATION OF INDIVIDUAL	FINGERPRINT AND OTHER INFORMATION	NOTARY FEE
		1	$
		2	$
		3	$
		4	$
		5	$
			$
			$
			$
			$
			$
			$
			$
			$
			$
			$
			$
			$
			$

Sample Page

Page 1	DATE NOTARIZED	TYPE OF NOTARIZATION	DATE OF DOCUMENT	TYPE OF DOCUMENT	SIGNATURE OF INDIVIDUAL	
					PRINTED	SIGNATURE
1						
2						
3						
4						
5						
6						
7						
8						
9						
10						
11						
12						
13						
14						
15						
16						
17						
18						
19						
20	DATE NOTARIZED	TYPE OF NOTARIZATION	DATE OF DOCUMENT	TYPE OF DOCUMENT	SIGNATURE OF INDIVIDUAL PRINTED	SIGNATURE

ADDRESS OF INDIVIDUAL	DETAILED IDENTIFICATION OF INDIVIDUAL	FINGERPRINT AND OTHER INFORMATION	NOTARY FEE
		1	$
		2	$
		3	$
		4	$
		5	$
		6	$
		7	$
		8	$
		9	$
		10	$
		11	$
		12	$
		13	$
		14	$
		15	$
		16	$
		17	$
		18	$
		19	$
		20	$

Page 2	DATE NOTARIZED	TYPE OF NOTARIZATION	DATE OF DOCUMENT	TYPE OF DOCUMENT	SIGNATURE OF INDIVIDUAL	
					PRINTED	SIGNATURE
1						
2						
3						
4						
5						
6						
7						
8						
9						
10						
11						
12						
13						
14						
15						
16						
17						
18						
19						
20						

ADDRESS OF INDIVIDUAL	DETAILED IDENTIFICATION OF INDIVIDUAL	FINGERPRINT AND OTHER INFORMATION	NOTARY FEE
		1	$
		2	$
		3	$
		4	$
		5	$
		6	$
		7	$
		8	$
		9	$
		10	$
		11	$
		12	$
		13	$
		14	$
		15	$
		16	$
		17	$
		18	$
		19	$
		20	$

Page 3	DATE NOTARIZED	TYPE OF NOTARIZATION	DATE OF DOCUMENT	TYPE OF DOCUMENT	SIGNATURE OF INDIVIDUAL	
					PRINTED	SIGNATURE
1						
2						
3						
4						
5						
6						
7						
8						
9						
10						
11						
12						
13						
14						
15						
16						
17						
18						
19						
20	DATE NOTARIZED	TYPE OF NOTARIZATION	DATE OF DOCUMENT	TYPE OF DOCUMENT	PRINTED	SIGNATURE

ADDRESS OF INDIVIDUAL	DETAILED IDENTIFICATION OF INDIVIDUAL	FINGERPRINT AND OTHER INFORMATION	NOTARY FEE
		1	$
		2	$
		3	$
		4	$
		5	$
		6	$
		7	$
		8	$
		9	$
		10	$
		11	$
		12	$
		13	$
		14	$
		15	$
		16	$
		17	$
		18	$
		19	$
		20	$

Page 4	DATE NOTARIZED	TYPE OF NOTARIZATION	DATE OF DOCUMENT	TYPE OF DOCUMENT	SIGNATURE OF INDIVIDUAL	
					PRINTED	SIGNATURE
1						
2						
3						
4						
5						
6						
7						
8						
9						
10						
11						
12						
13						
14						
15						
16						
17						
18						
19						
20						

ADDRESS OF INDIVIDUAL	DETAILED IDENTIFICATION OF INDIVIDUAL	FINGERPRINT AND OTHER INFORMATION	NOTARY FEE
		1	$
		2	$
		3	$
		4	$
		5	$
		6	$
		7	$
		8	$
		9	$
		10	$
		11	$
		12	$
		13	$
		14	$
		15	$
		16	$
		17	$
		18	$
		19	$
		20	$

Page 5	DATE NOTARIZED	TYPE OF NOTARIZATION	DATE OF DOCUMENT	TYPE OF DOCUMENT	SIGNATURE OF INDIVIDUAL	
					PRINTED	SIGNATURE
1						
2						
3						
4						
5						
6						
7						
8						
9						
10						
11						
12						
13						
14						
15						
16						
17						
18						
19						
20						

ADDRESS OF INDIVIDUAL	DETAILED IDENTIFICATION OF INDIVIDUAL	FINGERPRINT AND OTHER INFORMATION	NOTARY FEE
		1	$
		2	$
		3	$
		4	$
		5	$
		6	$
		7	$
		8	$
		9	$
		10	$
		11	$
		12	$
		13	$
		14	$
		15	$
		16	$
		17	$
		18	$
		19	$
		20	$

Page 6	DATE NOTARIZED	TYPE OF NOTARIZATION	DATE OF DOCUMENT	TYPE OF DOCUMENT	SIGNATURE OF INDIVIDUAL	
					PRINTED	SIGNATURE
1						
2						
3						
4						
5						
6						
7						
8						
9						
10						
11						
12						
13						
14						
15						
16						
17						
18						
19						
20						

ADDRESS OF INDIVIDUAL	DETAILED IDENTIFICATION OF INDIVIDUAL	FINGERPRINT AND OTHER INFORMATION	NOTARY FEE
		1	$
		2	$
		3	$
		4	$
		5	$
		6	$
		7	$
		8	$
		9	$
		10	$
		11	$
		12	$
		13	$
		14	$
		15	$
		16	$
		17	$
		18	$
		19	$
		20	$

Page 7	DATE NOTARIZED	TYPE OF NOTARIZATION	DATE OF DOCUMENT	TYPE OF DOCUMENT	SIGNATURE OF INDIVIDUAL	
					PRINTED	SIGNATURE
1						
2						
3						
4						
5						
6						
7						
8						
9						
10						
11						
12						
13						
14						
15						
16						
17						
18						
19						
20						

ADDRESS OF INDIVIDUAL	DETAILED IDENTIFICATION OF INDIVIDUAL	FINGERPRINT AND OTHER INFORMATION	NOTARY FEE
		1	$
		2	$
		3	$
		4	$
		5	$
		6	$
		7	$
		8	$
		9	$
		10	$
		11	$
		12	$
		13	$
		14	$
		15	$
		16	$
		17	$
		18	$
		19	$
		20	$

Page 8	DATE NOTARIZED	TYPE OF NOTARIZATION	DATE OF DOCUMENT	TYPE OF DOCUMENT	SIGNATURE OF INDIVIDUAL	
					PRINTED	SIGNATURE
1						
2						
3						
4						
5						
6						
7						
8						
9						
10						
11						
12						
13						
14						
15						
16						
17						
18						
19						
20						

ADDRESS OF INDIVIDUAL	DETAILED IDENTIFICATION OF INDIVIDUAL	FINGERPRINT AND OTHER INFORMATION	NOTARY FEE
		1	$
		2	$
		3	$
		4	$
		5	$
		6	$
		7	$
		8	$
		9	$
		10	$
		11	$
		12	$
		13	$
		14	$
		15	$
		16	$
		17	$
		18	$
		19	$
		20	$

Page 9	DATE NOTARIZED	TYPE OF NOTARIZATION	DATE OF DOCUMENT	TYPE OF DOCUMENT	SIGNATURE OF INDIVIDUAL	
					PRINTED	SIGNATURE
1						
2						
3						
4						
5						
6						
7						
8						
9						
10						
11						
12						
13						
14						
15						
16						
17						
18						
19						
20						

ADDRESS OF INDIVIDUAL	DETAILED IDENTIFICATION OF INDIVIDUAL	FINGERPRINT AND OTHER INFORMATION	NOTARY FEE
		1	$
		2	$
		3	$
		4	$
		5	$
		6	$
		7	$
		8	$
		9	$
		10	$
		11	$
		12	$
		13	$
		14	$
		15	$
		16	$
		17	$
		18	$
		19	$
		20	$

Page 10	DATE NOTARIZED	TYPE OF NOTARIZATION	DATE OF DOCUMENT	TYPE OF DOCUMENT	SIGNATURE OF INDIVIDUAL	
					PRINTED	SIGNATURE
1						
2						
3						
4						
5						
6						
7						
8						
9						
10						
11						
12						
13						
14						
15						
16						
17						
18						
19						
20	DATE NOTARIZED	TYPE OF NOTARIZATION	DATE OF DOCUMENT	TYPE OF DOCUMENT	PRINTED	SIGNATURE

ADDRESS OF INDIVIDUAL	DETAILED IDENTIFICATION OF INDIVIDUAL	FINGERPRINT AND OTHER INFORMATION	NOTARY FEE
		1	$
		2	$
		3	$
		4	$
		5	$
		6	$
		7	$
		8	$
		9	$
		10	$
		11	$
		12	$
		13	$
		14	$
		15	$
		16	$
		17	$
		18	$
		19	$
		20	$

Page 11	DATE NOTARIZED	TYPE OF NOTARIZATION	DATE OF DOCUMENT	TYPE OF DOCUMENT	SIGNATURE OF INDIVIDUAL	
					PRINTED	SIGNATURE
1						
2						
3						
4						
5						
6						
7						
8						
9						
10						
11						
12						
13						
14						
15						
16						
17						
18						
19						
20						

ADDRESS OF INDIVIDUAL	DETAILED IDENTIFICATION OF INDIVIDUAL	FINGERPRINT AND OTHER INFORMATION	NOTARY FEE
		1	$
		2	$
		3	$
		4	$
		5	$
		6	$
		7	$
		8	$
		9	$
		10	$
		11	$
		12	$
		13	$
		14	$
		15	$
		16	$
		17	$
		18	$
		19	$
		20	$

Page 12	DATE NOTARIZED	TYPE OF NOTARIZATION	DATE OF DOCUMENT	TYPE OF DOCUMENT	SIGNATURE OF INDIVIDUAL	
					PRINTED	SIGNATURE
1						
2						
3						
4						
5						
6						
7						
8						
9						
10						
11						
12						
13						
14						
15						
16						
17						
18						
19						
20	DATE NOTARIZED	TYPE OF NOTARIZATION	DATE OF DOCUMENT	TYPE OF DOCUMENT	SIGNATURE OF INDIVIDUAL	
					PRINTED	SIGNATURE

ADDRESS OF INDIVIDUAL	DETAILED IDENTIFICATION OF INDIVIDUAL	FINGERPRINT AND OTHER INFORMATION	NOTARY FEE
		1	$
		2	$
		3	$
		4	$
		5	$
		6	$
		7	$
		8	$
		9	$
		10	$
		11	$
		12	$
		13	$
		14	$
		15	$
		16	$
		17	$
		18	$
		19	$
		20	$

Page 13	DATE NOTARIZED	TYPE OF NOTARIZATION	DATE OF DOCUMENT	TYPE OF DOCUMENT	SIGNATURE OF INDIVIDUAL	
					PRINTED	SIGNATURE
1						
2						
3						
4						
5						
6						
7						
8						
9						
10						
11						
12						
13						
14						
15						
16						
17						
18						
19						
20						

ADDRESS OF INDIVIDUAL	DETAILED IDENTIFICATION OF INDIVIDUAL	FINGERPRINT AND OTHER INFORMATION	NOTARY FEE
		1	$
		2	$
		3	$
		4	$
		5	$
		6	$
		7	$
		8	$
		9	$
		10	$
		11	$
		12	$
		13	$
		14	$
		15	$
		16	$
		17	$
		18	$
		19	$
		20	$

Page 14	DATE NOTARIZED	TYPE OF NOTARIZATION	DATE OF DOCUMENT	TYPE OF DOCUMENT	SIGNATURE OF INDIVIDUAL	
					PRINTED	SIGNATURE
1						
2						
3						
4						
5						
6						
7						
8						
9						
10						
11						
12						
13						
14						
15						
16						
17						
18						
19						
20	DATE NOTARIZED	TYPE OF NOTARIZATION	DATE OF DOCUMENT	TYPE OF DOCUMENT	PRINTED	SIGNATURE

ADDRESS OF INDIVIDUAL	DETAILED IDENTIFICATION OF INDIVIDUAL	FINGERPRINT AND OTHER INFORMATION	NOTARY FEE
		1	$
		2	$
		3	$
		4	$
		5	$
		6	$
		7	$
		8	$
		9	$
		10	$
		11	$
		12	$
		13	$
		14	$
		15	$
		16	$
		17	$
		18	$
		19	$
		20	$

Page 15	DATE NOTARIZED	TYPE OF NOTARIZATION	DATE OF DOCUMENT	TYPE OF DOCUMENT	SIGNATURE OF INDIVIDUAL	
					PRINTED	SIGNATURE
1						
2						
3						
4						
5						
6						
7						
8						
9						
10						
11						
12						
13						
14						
15						
16						
17						
18						
19						
20						

ADDRESS OF INDIVIDUAL	DETAILED IDENTIFICATION OF INDIVIDUAL	FINGERPRINT AND OTHER INFORMATION	NOTARY FEE
		1	$
		2	$
		3	$
		4	$
		5	$
		6	$
		7	$
		8	$
		9	$
		10	$
		11	$
		12	$
		13	$
		14	$
		15	$
		16	$
		17	$
		18	$
		19	$
		20	$

Page 16	DATE NOTARIZED	TYPE OF NOTARIZATION	DATE OF DOCUMENT	TYPE OF DOCUMENT	SIGNATURE OF INDIVIDUAL	
					PRINTED	SIGNATURE
1						
2						
3						
4						
5						
6						
7						
8						
9						
10						
11						
12						
13						
14						
15						
16						
17						
18						
19						
20	DATE NOTARIZED	TYPE OF NOTARIZATION	DATE OF DOCUMENT	TYPE OF DOCUMENT	PRINTED	SIGNATURE

ADDRESS OF INDIVIDUAL	DETAILED IDENTIFICATION OF INDIVIDUAL	FINGERPRINT AND OTHER INFORMATION	NOTARY FEE
		1	$
		2	$
		3	$
		4	$
		5	$
		6	$
		7	$
		8	$
		9	$
		10	$
		11	$
		12	$
		13	$
		14	$
		15	$
		16	$
		17	$
		18	$
		19	$
		20	$

Page 17	DATE NOTARIZED	TYPE OF NOTARIZATION	DATE OF DOCUMENT	TYPE OF DOCUMENT	SIGNATURE OF INDIVIDUAL	
					PRINTED	SIGNATURE
1						
2						
3						
4						
5						
6						
7						
8						
9						
10						
11						
12						
13						
14						
15						
16						
17						
18						
19						
20	DATE NOTARIZED	TYPE OF NOTARIZATION	DATE OF DOCUMENT	TYPE OF DOCUMENT	PRINTED	SIGNATURE

ADDRESS OF INDIVIDUAL	DETAILED IDENTIFICATION OF INDIVIDUAL	FINGERPRINT AND OTHER INFORMATION	NOTARY FEE
		1	$
		2	$
		3	$
		4	$
		5	$
		6	$
		7	$
		8	$
		9	$
		10	$
		11	$
		12	$
		13	$
		14	$
		15	$
		16	$
		17	$
		18	$
		19	$
		20	$

Page 18	DATE NOTARIZED	TYPE OF NOTARIZATION	DATE OF DOCUMENT	TYPE OF DOCUMENT	SIGNATURE OF INDIVIDUAL	
					PRINTED	SIGNATURE
1						
2						
3						
4						
5						
6						
7						
8						
9						
10						
11						
12						
13						
14						
15						
16						
17						
18						
19						
20	DATE NOTARIZED	TYPE OF NOTARIZATION	DATE OF DOCUMENT	TYPE OF DOCUMENT	PRINTED	SIGNATURE

ADDRESS OF INDIVIDUAL	DETAILED IDENTIFICATION OF INDIVIDUAL	FINGERPRINT AND OTHER INFORMATION	NOTARY FEE
		1	$
		2	$
		3	$
		4	$
		5	$
		6	$
		7	$
		8	$
		9	$
		10	$
		11	$
		12	$
		13	$
		14	$
		15	$
		16	$
		17	$
		18	$
		19	$
		20	$

Page 19	DATE NOTARIZED	TYPE OF NOTARIZATION	DATE OF DOCUMENT	TYPE OF DOCUMENT	SIGNATURE OF INDIVIDUAL	
					PRINTED	SIGNATURE
1						
2						
3						
4						
5						
6						
7						
8						
9						
10						
11						
12						
13						
14						
15						
16						
17						
18						
19						
20						

ADDRESS OF INDIVIDUAL	DETAILED IDENTIFICATION OF INDIVIDUAL	FINGERPRINT AND OTHER INFORMATION	NOTARY FEE
		1	$
		2	$
		3	$
		4	$
		5	$
		6	$
		7	$
		8	$
		9	$
		10	$
		11	$
		12	$
		13	$
		14	$
		15	$
		16	$
		17	$
		18	$
		19	$
		20	$

Page 20	DATE NOTARIZED	TYPE OF NOTARIZATION	DATE OF DOCUMENT	TYPE OF DOCUMENT	SIGNATURE OF INDIVIDUAL	
					PRINTED	SIGNATURE
1						
2						
3						
4						
5						
6						
7						
8						
9						
10						
11						
12						
13						
14						
15						
16						
17						
18						
19						
20					PRINTED	SIGNATURE

ADDRESS OF INDIVIDUAL	DETAILED IDENTIFICATION OF INDIVIDUAL	FINGERPRINT AND OTHER INFORMATION	NOTARY FEE
		1	$
		2	$
		3	$
		4	$
		5	$
		6	$
		7	$
		8	$
		9	$
		10	$
		11	$
		12	$
		13	$
		14	$
		15	$
		16	$
		17	$
		18	$
		19	$
		20	$

Page 21	DATE NOTARIZED	TYPE OF NOTARIZATION	DATE OF DOCUMENT	TYPE OF DOCUMENT	SIGNATURE OF INDIVIDUAL	
					PRINTED	SIGNATURE
1						
2						
3						
4						
5						
6						
7						
8						
9						
10						
11						
12						
13						
14						
15						
16						
17						
18						
19						
20						

ADDRESS OF INDIVIDUAL	DETAILED IDENTIFICATION OF INDIVIDUAL	FINGERPRINT AND OTHER INFORMATION	NOTARY FEE
		1	$
		2	$
		3	$
		4	$
		5	$
		6	$
		7	$
		8	$
		9	$
		10	$
		11	$
		12	$
		13	$
		14	$
		15	$
		16	$
		17	$
		18	$
		19	$
		20	$

Page 22	DATE NOTARIZED	TYPE OF NOTARIZATION	DATE OF DOCUMENT	TYPE OF DOCUMENT	SIGNATURE OF INDIVIDUAL	
					PRINTED	SIGNATURE
1						
2						
3						
4						
5						
6						
7						
8						
9						
10						
11						
12						
13						
14						
15						
16						
17						
18						
19						
20						

ADDRESS OF INDIVIDUAL	DETAILED IDENTIFICATION OF INDIVIDUAL	FINGERPRINT AND OTHER INFORMATION	NOTARY FEE
		1	$
		2	$
		3	$
		4	$
		5	$
		6	$
		7	$
		8	$
		9	$
		10	$
		11	$
		12	$
		13	$
		14	$
		15	$
		16	$
		17	$
		18	$
		19	$
		20	$

Page 23	DATE NOTARIZED	TYPE OF NOTARIZATION	DATE OF DOCUMENT	TYPE OF DOCUMENT	SIGNATURE OF INDIVIDUAL	
					PRINTED	SIGNATURE
1						
2						
3						
4						
5						
6						
7						
8						
9						
10						
11						
12						
13						
14						
15						
16						
17						
18						
19						
20						

ADDRESS OF INDIVIDUAL	DETAILED IDENTIFICATION OF INDIVIDUAL	FINGERPRINT AND OTHER INFORMATION	NOTARY FEE
		1	$
		2	$
		3	$
		4	$
		5	$
		6	$
		7	$
		8	$
		9	$
		10	$
		11	$
		12	$
		13	$
		14	$
		15	$
		16	$
		17	$
		18	$
		19	$
		20	$

Page 24	DATE NOTARIZED	TYPE OF NOTARIZATION	DATE OF DOCUMENT	TYPE OF DOCUMENT	SIGNATURE OF INDIVIDUAL	
					PRINTED	SIGNATURE
1						
2						
3						
4						
5						
6						
7						
8						
9						
10						
11						
12						
13						
14						
15						
16						
17						
18						
19						
20						

ADDRESS OF INDIVIDUAL	DETAILED IDENTIFICATION OF INDIVIDUAL	FINGERPRINT AND OTHER INFORMATION	NOTARY FEE
		1	$
		2	$
		3	$
		4	$
		5	$
		6	$
		7	$
		8	$
		9	$
		10	$
		11	$
		12	$
		13	$
		14	$
		15	$
		16	$
		17	$
		18	$
		19	$
		20	$

Page 25	DATE NOTARIZED	TYPE OF NOTARIZATION	DATE OF DOCUMENT	TYPE OF DOCUMENT	SIGNATURE OF INDIVIDUAL	
					PRINTED	SIGNATURE
1						
2						
3						
4						
5						
6						
7						
8						
9						
10						
11						
12						
13						
14						
15						
16						
17						
18						
19						
20	DATE NOTARIZED	TYPE OF NOTARIZATION	DATE OF DOCUMENT	TYPE OF DOCUMENT	SIGNATURE OF INDIVIDUAL	
					PRINTED	SIGNATURE

ADDRESS OF INDIVIDUAL	DETAILED IDENTIFICATION OF INDIVIDUAL	FINGERPRINT AND OTHER INFORMATION	NOTARY FEE
		1	$
		2	$
		3	$
		4	$
		5	$
		6	$
		7	$
		8	$
		9	$
		10	$
		11	$
		12	$
		13	$
		14	$
		15	$
		16	$
		17	$
		18	$
		19	$
		20	$

Page 26	DATE NOTARIZED	TYPE OF NOTARIZATION	DATE OF DOCUMENT	TYPE OF DOCUMENT	SIGNATURE OF INDIVIDUAL	
					PRINTED	SIGNATURE
1						
2						
3						
4						
5						
6						
7						
8						
9						
10						
11						
12						
13						
14						
15						
16						
17						
18						
19						
20						

ADDRESS OF INDIVIDUAL	DETAILED IDENTIFICATION OF INDIVIDUAL	FINGERPRINT AND OTHER INFORMATION	NOTARY FEE
		1	$
		2	$
		3	$
		4	$
		5	$
		6	$
		7	$
		8	$
		9	$
		10	$
		11	$
		12	$
		13	$
		14	$
		15	$
		16	$
		17	$
		18	$
		19	$
		20	$

Page 27	DATE NOTARIZED	TYPE OF NOTARIZATION	DATE OF DOCUMENT	TYPE OF DOCUMENT	SIGNATURE OF INDIVIDUAL	
					PRINTED	SIGNATURE
1						
2						
3						
4						
5						
6						
7						
8						
9						
10						
11						
12						
13						
14						
15						
16						
17						
18						
19						
20						

ADDRESS OF INDIVIDUAL	DETAILED IDENTIFICATION OF INDIVIDUAL	FINGERPRINT AND OTHER INFORMATION	NOTARY FEE
		1	$
		2	$
		3	$
		4	$
		5	$
		6	$
		7	$
		8	$
		9	$
		10	$
		11	$
		12	$
		13	$
		14	$
		15	$
		16	$
		17	$
		18	$
		19	$
		20	$

Page 28	DATE NOTARIZED	TYPE OF NOTARIZATION	DATE OF DOCUMENT	TYPE OF DOCUMENT	SIGNATURE OF INDIVIDUAL	
					PRINTED	SIGNATURE
1						
2						
3						
4						
5						
6						
7						
8						
9						
10						
11						
12						
13						
14						
15						
16						
17						
18						
19						
20						

ADDRESS OF INDIVIDUAL	DETAILED IDENTIFICATION OF INDIVIDUAL	FINGERPRINT AND OTHER INFORMATION	NOTARY FEE
		1	$
		2	$
		3	$
		4	$
		5	$
		6	$
		7	$
		8	$
		9	$
		10	$
		11	$
		12	$
		13	$
		14	$
		15	$
		16	$
		17	$
		18	$
		19	$
		20	$

Page 29	DATE NOTARIZED	TYPE OF NOTARIZATION	DATE OF DOCUMENT	TYPE OF DOCUMENT	SIGNATURE OF INDIVIDUAL	
					PRINTED	SIGNATURE
1						
2						
3						
4						
5						
6						
7						
8						
9						
10						
11						
12						
13						
14						
15						
16						
17						
18						
19						
20						

ADDRESS OF INDIVIDUAL	DETAILED IDENTIFICATION OF INDIVIDUAL	FINGERPRINT AND OTHER INFORMATION	NOTARY FEE
		1	$
		2	$
		3	$
		4	$
		5	$
		6	$
		7	$
		8	$
		9	$
		10	$
		11	$
		12	$
		13	$
		14	$
		15	$
		16	$
		17	$
		18	$
		19	$
		20	$

Page 30	DATE NOTARIZED	TYPE OF NOTARIZATION	DATE OF DOCUMENT	TYPE OF DOCUMENT	SIGNATURE OF INDIVIDUAL	
					PRINTED	SIGNATURE
1						
2						
3						
4						
5						
6						
7						
8						
9						
10						
11						
12						
13						
14						
15						
16						
17						
18						
19						
20						

ADDRESS OF INDIVIDUAL	DETAILED IDENTIFICATION OF INDIVIDUAL	FINGERPRINT AND OTHER INFORMATION	NOTARY FEE
		1	$
		2	$
		3	$
		4	$
		5	$
		6	$
		7	$
		8	$
		9	$
		10	$
		11	$
		12	$
		13	$
		14	$
		15	$
		16	$
		17	$
		18	$
		19	$
		20	$

Page 31	DATE NOTARIZED	TYPE OF NOTARIZATION	DATE OF DOCUMENT	TYPE OF DOCUMENT	SIGNATURE OF INDIVIDUAL	
					PRINTED	SIGNATURE
1						
2						
3						
4						
5						
6						
7						
8						
9						
10						
11						
12						
13						
14						
15						
16						
17						
18						
19						
20						

ADDRESS OF INDIVIDUAL	DETAILED IDENTIFICATION OF INDIVIDUAL	FINGERPRINT AND OTHER INFORMATION	NOTARY FEE
		1	$
		2	$
		3	$
		4	$
		5	$
		6	$
		7	$
		8	$
		9	$
		10	$
		11	$
		12	$
		13	$
		14	$
		15	$
		16	$
		17	$
		18	$
		19	$
		20	$

IMPORTANT:

This record book of notarial acts
is required by state law, and must
not be destroyed.

If found, please return to the notary
public named on page